How to use this book

If you're reading this you obviously care about at least one child and want to **empower** them to deal with difficult situations. That's what **My Underpants RULE!** is made for! Although it is presented in a lighthearted way, it is designed around solid **principles of effective learning** so children can easily take away its very important message.

We know its content can be tricky to navigate as a reader, and how you deliver the message has an impact on the learning process. So here's some helpful advice to make your job easier.

Tip 1: Make it **fun and interactive**! Use the content to engage your child. Really ask the scenario questions, **let them think** before they answer, then move forward. Resist giving them the answers.

Tip 2: Repetition is one of the most important principles of early learning. Every time you come to **My Underpants RULE!** whether in full or in part, encourage your child to **repeat** each line after you. Work towards the point where they can say it at the same time as you and even better, **say it by themselves** (it's surprising how quickly they pick it up). When they can do that, you know they are well on the way to **My Underpants RULE!** being something they **remember for life**.

Tip 3: Similarly, read **My Underpants RULE!** with them regularly - once or twice a month. The more you read it together, the more its lessons will stay with your child.

Tip 4: Use the book to **create a conversation**. Over time your child may become curious about different aspects of the content, so **be guided by your child** on how far they need to go into a subject (which also makes it easier for you).

Tip 5: Talk to others about how you're using the book. Share tips between each other to gain inspiration. Visit our website **www.myunderpantsrule.com** for more ideas.

My Underpants RULE! is not a guarantee your child will avoid difficult situations. However, education is the first step in **empowerment**. At the very least, you will forewarn your child of potential dangers without unnecessarily alarming them, and reinforce the importance of **speaking to someone they trust** should anything happen. As parents ourselves, we hope your child never needs to.

Kate & Rod Power

Published by Kids Rule Publishing, Sydney Australia

For further enquiries or to join the movement, please visit:

www.Myunderpantsrule.com

Designed and set by Kids Rule Publishing

ISBN 978-0-9929530-0-3

Kids Rule Publishing

Kate & Rod Power

Don't you think it's rather silly

Don't you feel it's something strange...

How the things inside your underpants have lots of FUNNY naMes!

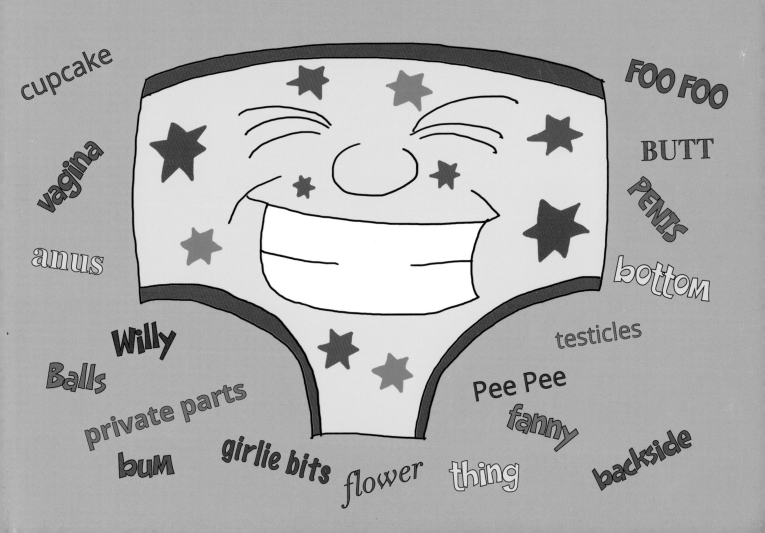

Don't you think it's even stranger
They make funny noises too?

brrp

Yes, you know we're talking about
The things that fart and pee and poop!

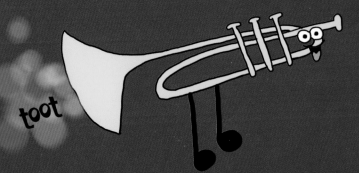

toot

tinkle

But though these things are funny
We must be careful with their use
'Coz they're important to our body
And everything we do

It's good to know their proper names
And protect them all the time
So follow the Underpants RULE!
And LEARN this simple rhyme

What's under my pants belongs
ONLY to ME!
And others CAN'T TOUCH there
or ask me to SEE

But SAFE grown-up or doctor
when I'm
NOT HEALTHY

What's under my pants
belongs
ONLY to ME!

My Underpants RULE!

And if this rule's BROKEN
I can RUN KICK or SCREAM

Yes it's really OK
if I make a BIG SCENE

My Underpants RULE!
has been BROKEN
you see

What's under my pants belongs
ONLY to ME!

So now you know the Underpants RULE!

Let's play a little game

Imagine these things happen

And tell me how you'd behave...

But remember as we do this

These probably won't come true

It's just important to be

READY

In case they ever do

Question 1:

Imagine someone bigger

Asks to see under your pants

What's the

Underpants RULE! tell you?

Ask for an answer before turning the page!

Should you give them any chance?

NO! NO! NO!

What's under my pants belongs
ONLY to ME
And others CAN'T TOUCH there
Or ask me to SEE!

Question 2:
What if someone puts their hand on you and TOUCHES your private parts???
Would you let them do it???

Ask for an answer before turning the page!

Or would you use your Underpants SMARTS?

NO! NO! NO!

And if this rule's BROKEN
I can RUN
KICK, or
SCREAM

Yes it's really OK
if I make a BIG SCENE

My Underpants RULE! has been
BROKEN you see

What's under my pants belongs ONLY to ME!

Question 3:

Now what if you're having **trouble**

With your farts,

poops

or pees?

Or you're sore
under your pants
Should anyone **touch or see?**

Ask for an
answer before
turning the page!

Question 4:

What if someone shows you the parts under their pants,

Ask for an answer before turning the page!

Or asks you to touch there Should you say "yes" or say "NO THANKS !?!?"

NO! NO! NO!

What's under THEIR pants belongs ONLY to THEM
So looking or touching
Breaks THEIR RULE! Again,
It's probably time to KICK, SCREAM or RUN
And straight away make sure you tell someone!

Question 5:

Finally, what if just by ACCIDENT Your private parts get touched?

Or someone sees you just by chance? Should you worry all that Much?

Ask for an answer before turning the page!

Well...
Accidents CAN happen when we wrestle, run or play
And we HAVE to take our clothes off
To wash ourselves each day

So the answer all depends
On how OK you FEEL

If you EVER feel that something's
WRONG
That's when you make a
BIG DEAL!

And if **ANY** of these things happen
ALWAYS tell someone you **TRUST**
Who wasn't there when it **HAPPENED**
And they'll help you work it out

It seems to me
you're
CLEVER

Because you
know now
what to do
But if ever you're
unsure

Just
remember
the
Underpants
RULE!